CHIEF JOSEPH

By R. P. Johnson

DILLON PRESS, INC.
MINNEAPOLIS, MINNESOTA

Dillon Press, Inc., 500 South Third Street
Minneapolis, Minnesota 55415

Printed in the United States of America

Library of Congress Cataloging in Publication Data

Johnson, Robert Proctor, 1924-
  Chief Joseph.
  (The Story of an American Indian)
  SUMMARY: A biography of the nineteenth-century
Nez Perce chief concentrating on his unending struggle
to win peace and equality for his people.
  1. Joseph, Nez Perce chief, 1840-1904 — Juvenile
literature. [1. Joseph, Nez Perce chief, 1840-1904. 2. Nez
Perce Indians — Biography. 3. Indians of North America
— Biography] I. Title.
E99.N5J585   970.3 [B]   74-11467
ISBN 0-87518-062-0

ON THE COVER:
*Chief Joseph as photographed by
F. J. Haynes in 1877.*

CHIEF JOSEPH

The Nez Perce War of 1877 was the last serious clash between the United States government and the native Americans. The history of this military adventure begins and ends with the seventeen-hundred-mile retreat by those Nez Perce Indians who refused to surrender their lands to the white settlers, ranchers, and miners. From the middle of June until early October, the Indians were overtaken and forced to engage in five important battles, in all but one of which they were triumphant. They assaulted or were attacked by enemy war parties in eleven lesser actions.

Out of these struggles emerged a leader of exceptional nobility and heroism. Chief Joseph was called upon by the tragedy of his time to become a fighter in war and the guide of a wandering and suffering people. And that tragedy was of a depth and extent to call forth the best qualities in a wise, good, and brave man.

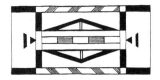

Contents

I THE ANGER OF THE DOVE page 1

II FENCES, PLOWS, AND RIFLES page 9

III FRIENDS INTO FOES page 25

IV ONE WARNING TOO LATE page 33

V THORNS AND ROSES page 43

VI FROM THE GARDEN TO THE GRAVE page 50

VII DEFEAT WITHOUT DISHONOR page 58

CHAPTER I

The Anger of the Dove

They climbed slowly, for the canyon trail was steep, their horses were burdened, and their hearts were heavy.

There were eight in the party: six men, one woman, and a girl. The men followed one another up the trail in single file. Each was leading a long string of pack horses. Across the backs of the horses lay the meat of the cattle that they had butchered.

The girl, Hophoponmi, led the way. For thirteen summers her cheerful spirit had brought happiness to her father and mother. But she was not cheerful now.

The warm morning sunlight and the fresh June breezes invited her to race the wild wind across the mountain meadow. But now she felt as though never again would she run with the free and happy wind.

Her family and her people had been driven from their homes in the Wallowa Valley. The white men had forced them to leave their beautiful Valley of Winding Waters. The old people, the women, and the children were very sad. The warriors were filled with anger and hatred.

Hophoponmi's father walked behind her. He was six feet tall and as strong as the buffalo. The white men called him Joseph, but he was known to his people by his rightful name, Hinmaton-yalatkit, the Numipu word for the thunder that traveled across the water and up over the land.

Following him were his brother, Ollokot, and Ollokot's wife, Fair-land. Ollokot was inches taller than Joseph, and almost as thin as a tepee pole. His step was nimble and quick. He was forever on the watch for excitement.

Joseph walked with the slow firm step of the proud chief. He had learned the habits of caution, long thought, and careful speech and action. For on his guidance depended the health and safety of two hundred people.

He was the chief of the Wellamotkin band of the Numipu tribe. His homeland, the Wallowa Valley, lay along the eastern border of what is now Oregon. It had been the last of the Numipu lands to be invaded by the white men, for it was bounded by the lofty Blue Mountains and by the deep canyons and boiling waters of the Snake River. For many years the white men had explored and settled the territory outside of these boundaries. Then rumors and curiosity about the Wallowa Valley overcame their fears, and they crossed the angry Snake River to investigate.

There they discovered the largest, the wealthiest, the strongest, and at the same time the friendliest and most generous of all the bands of the Numipu tribe. And the Numipu tribe was the largest and most powerful of all the tribes throughout the Northwest.

The men of the Numipu were known for their strength and courage, and the women for their beauty and reserve. All of the people were known for their intelligence, energy, and skills.

The white men knew them as the Nez Perces, which

Hinmaton-yalatkit,
photographer and date not recorded

means "pierced noses" in the French language. It had once been a custom among some of the Indians of this region to wear a decoration in the nose. The early French fur trappers thought that the ornament passed through the skin to hold it in place. Even though they were mistaken, and the custom was long since given up, the name continued to be used by the white men.

At last Chief Joseph and his party with their pack horses reached the end of their hard climb up the canyon trail. The way was more open now, and the land rose gradually to the encampment at Tepahlewam on Camas Prairie.

As Joseph and his hunting party approached the great meadow and came in sight of the camp which they had left only a short time before, a strange scene presented itself to them. There was confusion everywhere. Only a few tepees remained standing, and these were shaking and shivering like old men caught out in a winter storm, as the leather walls of the tepees were stripped from the supporting poles, and the poles were loosened from their ties.

A warrior on horseback came toward them at a gallop. He wore only his breechcloth and his moccasins. His face was painted in the colors of night and of blood. His dress and makeup were those of a man prepared to ride the path to war. The next moment, Two Moons brought his powerful horse to a thundering halt in front of Joseph.

He was an important member of Joseph's band, a fearsome warrior, an expert marksman, among the first of hunters, and an outspoken enemy of the white man. His dark eyes glistened in the flood of sunlight. A great excitement filled his spirit, but as any proud warrior should, he brought his feelings under control.

"It is good, Hinmaton-yalatkit, that you have butchered this meat," he said. "The women have harvested and stored the camas bulbs. This too is good. For the time has come when we shall need these stores of food and more. The time of war with the white man has come."

Two Moons went on to tell how that bold and skillful fighter, Wah-lait-its, had led two other young warriors in a search for Larry Ott, the white man who had murdered his father. Ott had escaped the vengeance of Wah-lait-its, but the three warriors had made other white men pay for his crime. Then a large group of young braves from White Bird's band had ridden out to join Wah-lait-its. Together, they were now hunting the white men who were guilty of so many terrible wrongs against the Nez Perces.

Old White Bird himself had taken his people back to their village in White Bird Canyon. Many of the white settlers there had fled their homes because of the killings by the braves.

As for the other chiefs, Toohoolhoolzote had gone with White Bird, and Looking Glass and Red Owl had returned to their villages. Looking Glass still hoped to live in peace on his land. The home of Red Owl, as Joseph knew, was within the boundaries of the new reservation. With or without a treaty, his people would not have to move.

Joseph had heard enough. He cast a look and a signal to Ollokot, and the two of them mounted their horses and rode off at a gallop across the prairie grass to the camp.

There, Joseph jumped from his horse and hurried in among the nervous old men, the frantic women, and the frightened children. He urged them to take heart, to remain where they were, that all would be well.

They had been shocked by the news that Wah-lait-its and his companions had murdered white men. Now they were further alarmed by the warriors of their own band who had stripped to their breechcloths and moccasins and painted their faces and decorated their horses in the colors of war. These young braves were now parading around the camp on their proud, high-stepping steeds and bellowing out the wild whoops that encouraged themselves and their friends to battle.

Ollokot was the leading hunter and fighter of the band. It was his task to guide and control the warriors. He stayed on his horse and raced about from one of the excited and noisy young braves to the next. He called out with a laugh to one, in anger to another, now with a joke, then with a snarl, whatever was most likely to cool each warrior's angry temper.

He soon persuaded them to calm their emotions. Only Two Moons with another very strong-minded and stubborn warrior left the camp and rode off to join Wah-lait-its.

Joseph moved among his people, quieting their fears. His manner was firm and yet gentle. His full voice carried his words to every ear, yet he did not command. He spoke as one to be trusted, not as one to be feared. He was dressed not for war, but for the peaceful labors of the camp. His broad shoulders and thick chest were clothed in a buckskin shirt, his powerful legs in buckskin leggings. The leggings, fastened to the leather belt of his breechcloth, reached from the breechcloth to the tops of his moccasins. By his appearance, his calm voice, and his confident manner, he brought relief and hope to his people.

That evening after dark he joined Hophoponmi in their

tepee. His wife was not there. She was lying on a soft bed of sheepskin in that special large tepee where only the women were allowed to go. She was about to give birth to a baby brother or sister for Hophoponmi.

After their evening meal, Hophoponmi lay down on her buffalo robe, with the roll of sheepskin for her head. Her father sat in the darkness at the far side of the tepee, alone with his thoughts.

He understood the bitterness of Wah-lait-its. A white man had murdered his father. His angry spirit had driven him to avenge his father's death. Joseph trembled with the fear that the very worst was about to happen to the Wella-motkin. He loved his life, his family, and his people. He wished with all his heart to return to his beloved Wallowa Valley, and he felt certain that someday he would return. And yet he would have given his life willingly if his death would have prevented a war with the white men.

Suddenly, the sound of galloping horses broke the silence of the night. Voices in the camp shouted cries of alarm and anger. The pounding hooves of the horses came very close. Joseph heard the scurry of the running feet of a warrior. The report of a rifle followed, and another, and then a volley of rifle shots. Suddenly a bullet tore through the wall of Joseph's tepee.

He called sharply to his daughter. Hophoponmi answered that she had not been hurt.

The shooting stopped and the sound of the horses' hooves died away with distance. Silence settled down again like the smothering of a crackling campfire.

Ollokot came to tell his brother Joseph that no one had been injured by the surprise attack. Joseph was thankful for this. But what of tomorrow? What was to come?

Like many of the warriors, the white men had been roused to seek vengeance. They had always feared and hated the Indians. Now Wah-lait-its and his friends had given them an excuse to destroy all the Nez Perces who refused to accept a permanent home on the reservation.

"We are not to blame," Ollokot said. "Nobody from the Wellamotkin band took part in the killings of the white men."

"Yes, we can go in safety and find peace on the reservation," said Joseph. "And if we choose to support White Bird, we may be leading our people to war. Which is the shorter path back to the Wallowa Valley, peace or war?"

The Nez Perces had been cheated, shamed, robbed, and murdered by the white men for more years than most of them had lived. They had been patient. They had returned kindness for injuries. They had met insults with silence. This was the way of the Nez Perce people. This was still their way, even though they knew the stories and could tell the names of the white murderers of no fewer than thirty of their people. And not one of these murderers had ever paid for his crime. Until now, never had a Nez Perce warrior taken the life of a single white brother.

"The white men promise the Indians a poor future," said Joseph. "Let us have peace so long as there is hope of returning to our homeland. When that hope is gone, then we will return by the path of war."

CHAPTER II

Fences, Plows,
and Rifles

In the early time, before the white man came with his fences and rifles to defend the square of ground he claimed as his own, peace and friendship were the laws that governed the hearts of men. Quarrels were short, justice was honest and swift, and enemies were no sooner defeated than they were forgiven. Then the land belonged to all men, and everyone enjoyed and shared the plenty of the earth, the rivers, and the forests.

Since ancient times, the Nez Perces had lived and prospered in the vast and wealthy region that is now the northeast corner of Oregon, the southeast corner of Washington, and all of central Idaho. This land of their livelihood and happiness reached from the Blue Mountains on the west to the Bitterroot Range on the east, and from the banks of the Clearwater River in the north to the canyons of the Salmon River in the south.

Their permanent homes were located in the low valleys near the mouths of good fishing streams. The floors of the houses were sunk about three feet below the ground, and the dirt that had been dug out was piled up on the four sides to form the lower half of the walls. The upper half of the walls and the roof were framed with logs, and the framework was covered by a thick, tight matting of plant stems sewn and bound with Indian hemp. Holes in the roof allowed the smoke of the cooking fires to escape.

So well-planned and well-constructed were these houses that during the winter season, when the entrances were closed against the weather, the people slept in comfort and warmth through even the bitterest cold of the longest winter nights.

During the winter months, their favorite pleasure was to call upon the neighbors. They loved society, and visits between families and villages were common.

Still, work was never neglected. The skill of many hands and the labor of many hours were needed to fashion the important and valuable articles of Nez Perce craftsmanship. The quality of their weaving was without equal. Their baskets, sacks, and other containers, woven of Indian hemp, were used for berry picking, food storage, and they also served as traveling bags. The containers were sturdy enough to serve a warrior and his bride all the days of their married life. The firm, close weaving of the best craftsmen produced baskets that could hold and carry water.

Remarkable also was the Nez Perce bow which was formed from the coiled horn of the mountain sheep. With heat, moisture, time, and muscle, the Nez Perces drew the spiral of the horn into a length of about three feet, and then attached a string of leather. Setting an arrow to the string, they could drop a running deer with such force that the bloody arrow, which was almost as long as the bow, would lie on the ground at some distance on the opposite side of the fallen animal. Until the white man's rifle entered the country, this bow was the prized weapon of all the tribes in the Northwest, and brought the price of a good horse in trade.

Horses were introduced into their country during the early years of the eighteenth century. By careful breeding of the horse the Nez Perces developed in time the famous spotted Appaloosa. In size and strength, in spirit, speed, and beauty, no other was a match for it. The white man willingly paid the highest price for such an animal. And as the climate and the grassland of the Nez Perce country were favorable to the raising of large herds, the selling and trading of their horses helped to make this tribe the richest in all the Northwest.

The Nez Perces left their winter homes early in the season of new growth to search for the cowish herb, an important source of food. The weather had only begun to turn mild, the snows to melt, and the ground to thaw. But already the earth of the lower meadows had brought the roots of the cowish herb to their full growth.

These roots were found and uncovered by stabbing with pointed sticks through the thin layer of wet snow and into the half-frozen mud. They were then collected in baskets, cleaned, and cooked into a porridge for present use and into biscuits to be stored for future needs.

After this harvest was completed late in the spring, the people again rounded up their horses and cattle, packed up their belongings, and moved on into the higher mountain slopes, here to harvest the sweet bulb of the camas plant.

The smaller fields of camas were harvested along the trail to one of the large meadows in the high country. Here the band made a permanent summer camp at one of the traditional gathering places of the tribe. Tepahlewam was a favorite site, where many families and often entire bands met to spend the warm and pleasant season together in horse racing, gambling, and gossip.

Firewood was plentiful and the clear flowing streams abounded in salmon and trout. The nearby trees and bushes hung heavy with berries and fruits, and the rich soil furnished wild onions, wild carrots, the bitterroot, and other foods.

Here the women continued the annual harvest of the camas bulbs. Their digging sticks for the camas had curved crosspieces on top for handles and were forked below to twist and lift the bulbs above the surface of the ground.

To labor in the fields, to cook, and to clean — these were the tasks of the women. Sometimes the men would help when the work was heavy, but their main occupations were fishing, hunting, and war. It was their job to set traps in the river and bring in the salmon, which furnished well over half their food supply. The men also faced the trials and dangers of the hunt, and upon each one depended the safety not only of his own family, but also of the band as a whole.

Later on during the summer, the fishermen lined the banks of the rivers. At a certain time of the year, great schools of salmon swam up the river, and the waters turned silver with their bodies. Then the fishermen went to work with their spears and nets, and the shores of the rivers and streams became alive with the flurry of the surprised and waterless fish.

The fish were hung on wood frames to be dried in the

Nez Perce woman making pemican

sun or laid on stones in the fire pits to be smoked. The smoking and the drying preserved the fish until winter.

With the first chill winds that signaled the change of season, the Nez Perces prepared to descend to their winter homes in the valleys below. Then began the task of packing and loading their stores of food and fish. There was additional work for those families whose men had been lucky on their hunting trips. Their pack horses were loaded with dried elk or deer meat.

The horse was more than a servant and a beast of burden. It was also a pet at home and a companion on the journey. And proud and respected was the warrior whose mount ran swiftest in the race or was cleverest on the hunt or most obedient on the warpath. But whether it served only to herd the cattle, pull the travois, or carry the heavy packs and supplies of meat, every horse was cared for and loved by the Nez Perces.

The early Nez Perces had taught their children to be kind and respectful toward everything that lived. Before Christianity came to their country, their religion had taught them to love and worship the earth as the mother of all life. Every plant and animal had been sacred to them. They had believed that it was wrong to harm any living thing, except to feed themselves. Many Indians still clung to these old beliefs. Most were members of a religious group known as Dreamers. They still thought that the white men were very sinful to drive away or kill the creatures of the field and then to wound the earth with the blades of their plows.

The year 1805 saw the first meeting of the Nez Perces and the white men. In September of that year, the expedition led by Meriwether Lewis and William Clark appeared on Weippe Prairie. They were weak from hunger after their difficult crossing of the long, rough Lolo Trail. The Nez Perces saved them from starvation.

The white strangers proved to be good men, gentle in their manners and respectful of the rights and feelings of others. William Clark was a doctor of medicine, and he cured or lessened the suffering of many Indians who were ill.

The medicine of the doctor was very good, but there were other wonders far more amazing. One of these was the rifle; another was the small round glass that could make fire with sunlight and dry twigs.

But most wonderful of all was the talking paper. And the curiosity of the intelligent Nez Perces made them very impatient to discover the mystery of those twin marvels called writing and reading.

In 1836, with the willing assistance of the Indians, a missionary named Henry Spalding built a church and school beside a small creek called Lapwai. Here he settled down to instruct the eager Nez Perces in the wonder of the written word.

Spalding looked upon the Indians as a poor and ignorant people who must be taught and trained in the knowledge, habits, and beliefs of the white men. For their own good, he felt, they must learn to be farmers, ranchers, carpenters, and Christians.

Each family was to live in one and the same house every day of the year. Every woman was to have her own kitchen. Every man was to have a plot of ground to call his own.

In return for these benefits of the white man's civilization, Spalding demanded that the children come every day to the church or the classroom, even during the time of spring harvest. He demanded that the warrior trade his hunting rifle for a hoe to weed the garden, and his saddle for a bucket to carry feed to the chickens and pigs.

The Nez Perces all wanted to learn how to read and write, but some of them could not understand why it was necessary to give up the traditions of their fathers. They asked how their own religion was different from the teachings of the white missionary. Did the Nez Perces not forgive their enemies? Did they not help the weak, the poor, and the sick? Were they not men of peace?

Spalding refused to hear such foolishness. The Indians must become Christians or he would not teach them how to use the talking paper. The white men were a superior people, he said, and possessed a thousand marvels because they knew how to read and write. And the Nez Perces did want to become the equals of the white men.

By 1839, only three years after Spalding built his church and school, more than a hundred Nez Perce families were living as Christians. The men worked in the gardens, the women cooked and cleaned in the houses, the children studied in the classroom, and everybody attended church on Sunday.

And in that year, Henry Spalding baptized the chief of the largest and wealthiest band of the Numipu tribe. The chief was Tuekakas, his band was the Wellamotkin, and they lived in the Wallowa Valley. Spalding baptized Tuekakas with the Christian name of Joseph. Tuekakas was the father of Hinmaton-yalatkit, who was then called Young Joseph by the white men, and who is the Chief Joseph of this story.

Young Joseph's father placed his trust in the charity of the Christians. But then other men with other purposes came after the missionary and his teachings. After him marched the white man's army. Roads were constructed and forts were built to house the soldiers whose numbers increased as more white settlers invaded the country.

Little by little, more and more of the land was fenced, plowed, and planted. Miles and miles of fences gave directions to the rider on horseback. And the hunter on the trail of the deer and elk had to ride farther and still farther to overtake the game.

The Nez Perces were patient with the visitors to their homeland. They still believed in the goodness of most white men. The memory of their past friendship with Lewis and Clark was still alive.

Traveling to the camas meadows or riding the hunting trails, they were careful not to disturb the white man's fences. But as in the old days, they allowed their cattle and horses to graze freely in the open pastures. Sometimes their herds became mixed with those of the white men. Before the animals could be separated, angry words passed between the owners. Often the white rancher would claim that the Indian's herd was part of his own. Many an Indian lost his life for calling a white cattle thief by his rightful name.

The fighting grew worse and the murders more frequent. At last the white leaders realized that their own people and the Indians must be protected from one another. In 1855, the governor of the Washington Territory, Isaac Stevens, called a council of all the tribes in the region.

The boundaries of a reservation were established.

Those Indians who lived outside the boundaries were to receive a payment for their land and a place to live on the reservation. Some of the chiefs gave up their rights to the land without an argument; others were forced to sell. Most of the Nez Perce homeland, including that of Young Joseph's father, lay within the borders of the reservation, so an outbreak of serious trouble was delayed.

Before the Treaty of 1855, white men had searched for gold in Nez Perce country. After the treaty, they crossed the reservation borders in secret, hidden by forests and canyon walls. In 1860, a rich mine of gold was found on the banks of a stream just north of the Clearwater River. Word of the discovery spread quickly to the white settlements. At once all the other prospectors in the territory demanded that the government and army give them the right and protection to invade the Nez Perce reservation. But whether or not they received permission, they were determined to have a share in that fortune of gold.

Again there were bitter quarrels, fighting, and the murder of Indians. Again the agents of the white man's government were called upon to act. They drew the new limits of another, smaller reservation.

By this time the office of an Indian agent and an army stockade had been built at Lapwai, near the church and school of Henry Spalding. The settlement was now called Fort Lapwai. To the southeast of the fort lay the land of the new reservation.

At the council meeting with the Nez Perces in 1863, the agents mapped out the new boundaries. Of every ten acres of the old reservation, nine were to be given to the white men, and one was to be left for the Indians.

Old Tuekakas stormed out of the council. Not he, nor his son, nor his son's son would ever give up the land of the Wellamotkin. They would remain in the Wallowa Valley forever.

Four other chiefs, almost as angry as Tuekakas, followed on his heels. White Bird, Looking Glass, Toohoolhoolzote, and Red Owl rejected the decision of the council.

For the rest of his life, Tuekakas refused to be called by his Christian name, Joseph. From that day until his death, he thundered his wrath against the thieves who had drawn up the Treaty of 1863, and raged against the cowardice of the chiefs who had signed it.

When he died in 1871, the settlers and ranchers immediately demanded his land. They ordered their government to drive the Indians out of the Wallowa Valley. But when the Indian agent told him to lead his people to the reservation, Young Joseph, now the chief of the Wellamotkin, replied with a firm no. The white men pleaded, argued, and threatened, but with quiet dignity, which was his manner, he always answered no.

> If we ever owned the land we own it still, for we never sold it. In the treaty councils the commissioners have claimed that our country had been sold to the government. Suppose a white man should come to me and say, "Joseph, I like your horses, and I want to buy them." I say to him, "No, my horses suit me, I will not sell them." Then he goes to my neighbor, and says to him, "Joseph has some good horses. I want to buy them, but he refuses to sell." My neighbor answers, "Pay me the money, and I will sell you Joseph's horses." The white man returns to me and says,

"Joseph, I have bought your horses, and you must let me have them." If we sold our lands to the government, this is the way they were bought.

A few white men, hearing his story, admired the courage of his stand in defense of his homeland. The story was told and repeated, until it reached the ears of the head chief of the white man's government in Washington, D.C. And so it happened that in 1873, President Grant signed an official declaration that set aside the Wallowa Valley as the property of the Wellamotkin band from that day forward and for all time.

The protests of the settlers and ranchers were heard like the howls of coyotes in the capital of the nation. The white men were moving into the Wallowa Valley in growing numbers. They met with Joseph, but only to argue with him. They insulted and threatened him and the warriors of his band. They hoped to cause one of them to lose his temper and begin a fight. This would give them an excuse to call in the soldiers to help them drive the Indians out of the valley.

Joseph remained calm. He was determined to avoid trouble. Ollokot kept the young warriors under control. The band went on living as before, though the settlers were turning more and more to violence against them. And in Washington, the friends of the settlers were howling louder than ever.

Finally, President Grant was persuaded to change his mind. Only two years after he had signed it, his declaration was scrapped.

To see that all of the Nez Perce were herded onto the new reservation, the white man's government sent General

Otis Howard to Fort Lapwai. Under the general's command were all the soldiers and weapons necessary to carry out his orders. Howard reported back to Washington, suggesting that Congress be asked to let the Indians keep the Valley. But this was not to be.

He told the chiefs to make their decision. The choice was up to them: either the reservation or war, Christianity or slavery, a garden plot or death. "But you must choose carefully," he said. "Is it not the duty of a chief to protect his people?"

The general spoke truly. The chief must save the people. Joseph's band was the largest and strongest of all the bands of the Nez Perce tribe. And Joseph himself, ever since he had become a chief, had been the first in councils to urge the tribe to resist the white men and remain on their lands. For these reasons, the settlers and their army would welcome the opportunity to make war on the Wellamotkin. In such a war, there would be much suffering and death for his people. They must continue to resist, but in another way. He would lead his people away from their homeland, but he would not surrender it, not in the way that the white men were demanding of him.

"Very well," said Joseph. "The Wellamotkin shall leave the Wallowa Valley, as every spring we leave for the camas meadows. The day when we will return, only the Great Spirit knows."

In a stern voice General Howard informed the chiefs that they had just thirty days in which to bring their people into the reservation.

"The Wellamotkin will need twice thirty days," Joseph said. The Snake River was running full. Its swift current was dangerous at any time of the year, but in the spring, as now, it was very treacherous. Often for a period of many days it was impossible to cross.

General Howard was very angry. "How dare you!" he cried. "You, an ignorant savage, how dare you look a white man straight in the eye and argue with him as an equal! You have ears. Use them. I repeat, thirty days, and not a day more. Inform your people. Everyone must appear within the Lapwai reservation by the middle of June. Any person who fails to do so shall feel the sting of an army rifle."

"Would the general begin a war?" Joseph asked.

"Of course not," said General Howard. "I am a man of peace. But my orders must be obeyed. I have my orders, too, and I must obey them."

Thirty days were a very short time for so difficult a task. The Indians must round up their herds of hundreds of cattle and thousands of horses. They must pack up all their possessions. They must build and borrow many rafts and canoes. The old people, the sick, the crippled, and the mothers with babies must be helped to strap themselves and their burdens first to their horses and then to the rafts. Then they must cross both the Snake and the Salmon rivers.

The Salmon River is wide and swift, and its canyon walls are steep. The gorge of the Snake River is one of the deepest on the North American continent. And now, in the middle of May, the waters of the melting snows were rushing down the mountainsides, swelling the streams that fed the mighty rivers and filling the deep river canyons with ugly, frothing torrents.

In the confusion and dangers of the move, the white men managed to steal many cattle from the Nez Perces. A number of horses were carried away in the current. There were narrow escapes, but everyone reached the far banks alive.

On the fourteenth day of June, 1877, with a full week of the thirty days still remaining, Chief Joseph and his band had climbed the steep trails to Tepahlewam. They were now within two days' journey of Fort Lapwai. Here they had joined the other bands who, until then, had also refused to leave their ancient lands. They all made camp to enjoy their last days of freedom.

But the warriors had found little pleasure in these final hours of their liberty. They had sat around the campfires and spoken in sad words of their past life, in bitter words of their coming imprisonment on the reservation, and in words of hatred for the white men who were putting them there.

After resting a few days, Joseph and Ollokot had left the camp, taking with them Ollokot's wife, Joseph's daughter, a party of four braves, and a string of pack horses for each man. They had followed a trail down into the canyon of the Salmon River, and had butchered cattle to feed the Wellamotkin band.

It was then that Wah-lait-its and his friends had taken the warpath, and white men had been killed. And now a war party of white men had attacked the camp, and sent a bullet through the wall of Joseph's tepee.

With the rising of the sun the next morning, the days of their freedom from the reservation were numbered with two fingers. Now those fingers had drawn the bowstring against the white men. And the white men had answered with their rifles. Were these the first steps down the path to war?

CHAPTER III

Friends
into Foes

When Joseph awoke, he learned that during the night his wife had given birth to a baby girl. He was both happy and worried. If war came, life would not be easy for the mothers with babies in their arms.

That morning Two Moons and his companion returned. The warriors were pleased, but the women greeted them with a cold silence.

The people broke camp and left the open prairie. They followed Joseph on the trail among the rolling hills in the direction of White Bird Creek. By late afternoon they arrived at the village of Chief White Bird.

A laughing, cheering crowd escorted them into the camp. Old Chief Toohoolhoolzote was perhaps the happiest one of all to welcome them.

He was tough and mean, as strong as a bear, and the terror of his enemies. His age of over sixty years hardly weighed upon him at all. Not long ago he had carried on his wide shoulders two full-grown deer, each encircled by one of his powerful arms.

He hated all white men and never grew weary of saying so. Once he had used insulting language to General Howard. At the general's command, five soldiers had succeeded in throwing the grumbling old grizzly bear into prison for the night. This experience had made Toohoolhoolzote very impatient to begin a war with the white men.

He was overjoyed when Joseph arrived, for with the Wellamotkin band rode more than fifty good fighting men. He himself led thirty braves. And when Wah-lait-its returned with the warriors of Chief White Bird's band, the Nez Perces would have a combined force of nearly one hundred men to take the field against the white man's army.

Joseph studied their position. The camp was protected on one side by a strong river. On the opposite side were the two steep hills that formed the canyon. The land was clear of trees and bushes, but the hills were topped by rocky ledges. Between the hills and the river, above and below the camp, were deep ravines and huge boulders which would hide and help defend the scouts and war parties.

To guard the camp during the night, warriors were sent into the hills. Those who had watched through the day came down for the evening meal and a few hours of sleep. Darkness fell and the campfires were put out. The young braves who had no scouting duties spaced themselves in a protective ring about the village of tepees.

The hours passed. A faint half-moon hung like a wet white feather in the black sky. It was the dead of night. Not a sound disturbed the camp. The people lay slumbering in their beds.

High up on one of the hills a match was struck to light a pipe. The next instant, out of the black stillness came the howl of the coyote.

The warriors in the tepees reached for their weapons.

They touched the women to warn them. The women hushed the children and held their babies close to quiet them.

That wail of the coyote had been made by one of the scouts. It was the signal that white men had been discovered in the hills.

The chiefs, the old men, and the warriors gathered under the dull light of the half-moon in an open area between the camp and the hills. They formed a circle. The chiefs and old men sat on buffalo robes. The warriors squatted down on their heels.

The council waited out of respect for old Chief White Bird to begin. His years were seventy, and his thoughts and his words were slow.

"Perhaps the white men bring a message of peace from General Howard," he said at last.

Toolhoolhoolzote raised his hand. He said that he wished to be heard. At this, the warriors laughed. It was funny to hear that old chief ask permission to speak. If he wanted to be heard, he only had to use his voice. If the buffalo had a tongue that could make words, it would speak exactly like Toohoolhoolzote.

"More messages?" he said angrily. "More meetings? More treaties? What good are these? The white man is like a child. He makes many promises but easily forgets them."

Joseph was the youngest and the last of the chiefs to speak. Although his years were but half those of White Bird, his wisdom had been tested, and the council listened carefully to all that he said.

If the white men come with an offer of peace, then let us have peace. For I fear that a war would destroy us all. To the white man, we are like the buffalo that would break down his fences and graze in his pastures, or the deer that would eat the green leaves in his garden. He would kill us all to save his grass and his beans.

"When in doubt, the wisest word is patience," said Chief White Bird.

Two Moons struck his knee with his fist. "What good is this talk?" he said. "White men have been killed by Nez Perce warriors. War has already broken out."

"Perhaps not," old White Bird said, "if our young braves would calm themselves and put the white man's fears to rest."

"Always we have gone the way of peace," said Toohoolhoolzote. "And our lands have been stolen and our warriors murdered. Now you say it is the fault of our young braves. An old chief ought to be wiser than that."

The debate continued until the first light of the new day. Then it was interrupted by hoofbeats. A scout came riding into the camp with the warning that everyone had been expecting. The soldiers were on the march. They were even now at the very brow of the hill.

The council appointed six warriors, under the leadership of Wetti Wetti, to ride out with the white flag of truce. They were to meet with the white chief and invite him to smoke the pipe of peace with the Nez Perce chiefs.

The Indians were equipped with bows and arrows, twelve old and damaged shotguns, and only three modern rifles like those carried by all of the white men. And yet without a moment's pause in doubt or fear, the warriors mounted their horses, joined one of the war parties or rode off alone, and disappeared into the ravines and among the rocks and hills.

About a hundred of the white men wore the uniform of the American army. Another twelve were dressed in the clothing of the men in the settlements. Ten of these volunteers took positions behind large rocks near the top of the hill. They were to guard the rear of the fighting men.

Half of the soldiers dismounted, leaving their horses with the ten volunteers. With their chief, Captain David Perry, in the lead, they began to move in single file on a path down the slope of the hill.

As they came down, the troops on foot spread out in a long line over the grassy curve of the land. The men on horseback rode off to the right and left to guard the two ends of this line. Every soldier was armed with a new rifle, and from his shoulder hung a long belt of ammunition.

Two of the soldiers carried trumpets. To command his long file of troops, the captain gave his order to one of these men, who then blew a series of notes on his horn, a different series for each of the different commands. In this way, the soldiers received their orders when they were marching or fighting on the field of battle at a distance from their captain.

Wetti Wetti, followed by the other members of his peace party, rode out to meet Captain Perry. From the top of a long pole resting on his saddle flew the white flag of truce.

One of the volunteers in Perry's company raised his rifle and fired twice at the Indians. The warriors reined their horses back away from the white men. None of them was struck by these first shots.

A warrior returned the fire, and a man with a trumpet

fell from his horse. He was the first man to die in the Battle of White Bird Canyon.

The next instant, Two Moons with a party of sixteen warriors started from behind a small cliff of rock and charged the ten volunteers on the top of the hill. The white men ran for cover.

At the same moment, Ollokot and his band of followers rushed from behind a hill. They dashed in among the troops on horseback. Their sudden appearance and wild shouting startled the soldiers and their animals alike. Some of the white men were thrown from their frightened horses. Others clung to the reins with one hand while trying to aim their rifles with the other. Their bullets went speeding toward the sky or into the ground, in every direction except the one that would have stopped an Indian.

The retreat of the volunteers on the hilltop left unguarded the soldiers who were fighting halfway down the hill. Two Moons and his braves now turned their attention and their arrows upon these troops.

Although they were many and the Indians few, the soldiers appeared to be surrounded by their foes. Their greater number counted for nothing in the terrible swift movement of the powerful Appaloosa mounts which were ridden with such skill and boldness by the Nez Perce horsemen.

Again the white men were scattered. Eighteen were driven against a cliff of rock and destroyed to the last man. Sixteen of the remaining troops were also killed. The rest gained the top of the hill and escaped.

The action had lasted only a few minutes, but it ended in a clear victory for the Nez Perces. The troops and volunteers had outnumbered the warriors by more than thirty men, and thirty-four white men, nearly one for every three of their entire war party, had been killed. Two of the Indian braves had been wounded, and not a single one had lost his life.

The young warriors shouted and boasted in their tri-

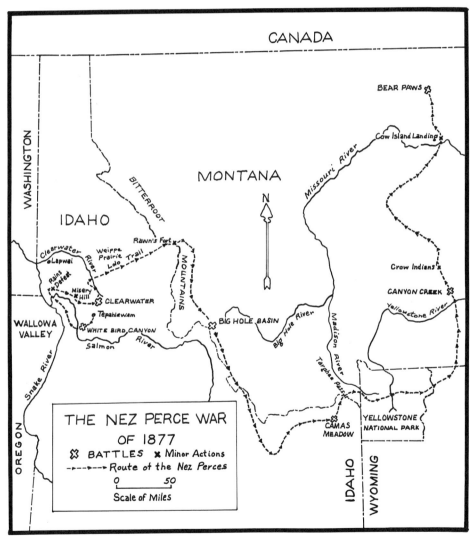

Map by R. P. Johnson

umph. The old warriors, who had taught the young, were proud of them and free with their praise.

At the next council there was no debate about war and peace. That decision had been made for them.

"If only there were some other way," said old Chief White Bird.

"When the soldiers come again, it will be in numbers many times a hundred," said one of the old men.

"Fifty brave warriors fighting for their homes can defeat a thousand thieves who fight only to steal the land," said Two Moons.

"The white man is worse than a thief," said Chief Toohoolhoolzote. "In his speech he is a man of peace, but in his actions he dishonors the white flag of truce. He is like a child who can speak his father's tongue but does not yet know the meaning of the words."

"Still," said Chief White Bird, "I do wish there were some other way."

A scout reported that Wah-lait-its and the other warriors of White Bird's band were camped in the woods on the other side of the river. They were not yet ready to receive the black looks and hard words from their chief. White Bird wondered if they realized the terrible evil that they had done. Joseph reminded him that it was not the warriors but the white men who had begun this war. In spite of this truth, it was with a sad and doubtful heart that the old chief forgave his angry young men.

CHAPTER IV

One Warning
Too Late

On the very morning after the Battle of White Bird Canyon, the hunting party led by Rainbow and Five Wounds returned from Montana. They came with exciting tales to tell of their adventures in the buffalo country. Instead, they listened while the fighting braves related the success of their first encounter with the United States army.

The council welcomed the advice of Rainbow and Five Wounds. These two were men of great experience. Their voice in council was equal to that of a chief. With their help, a plan was formed.

Thirty warriors were sent into the mountains to observe the actions of the white men. Led by Joseph, the rest of the tribe with their horses crossed to the west bank of the Salmon River. They climbed into the great hills of rock and forest and camped in a sheltered place on Deer Creek.

Day and night the scouts kept a constant and careful watch on the movements of the enemy. General Howard himself was out tracking them. He commanded a war party of over four hundred soldiers and twenty volunteers, with fifty other white men and thirty Indians to serve as guides and to lead the pack horses.

The white men prepared to cross the Salmon River in

pursuit of the Nez Perces. The crossing was not as easy as they had expected. The banks of the Salmon were steep and rocky, and its current was swift, though it was a tame and quiet stream compared to the torrent of the Snake River.

Howard's people were all men, all healthy, and most were young. The Indians had old people, women, and children to look out for. The soldiers had only themselves. When Joseph heard of their difficulties, he thought that perhaps General Howard might learn to have a little respect for the people he had called "the savages of the wilderness."

It was the seventh day after the tribe had left White Bird Canyon. High on a cliff above the Deer Creek camp, Yellow Wolf waved his red blanket. This was to signal that the white men were beginning to move their rafts and swim their horses across the Salmon River. Joseph told the people to break camp. They loaded their possessions onto the pack horses and followed him northward.

With the old and the sick, with four hundred women and children, and with thousands of horses moving through dense forests and over ragged peaks of mountain rock, Joseph managed to move the Nez Perces a full twenty-five miles in only a day and a half. At a turn in the Salmon River, they paused to wait for a signal from one of their scouts.

On the afternoon of the next day, the waving red blanket told them that all of the white men had passed to the west bank of the Salmon, at the place where the tribe had crossed ten days before. Then the chiefs directed their people to cross again to the other side of the river.

Howard and his troops followed the Nez Perces on the trail to the north. So rough and strange was the country for the white men that the same distance traveled by the Indians in one day and a half took Howard and his soldiers a full four days.

By this time the Nez Perces were well on their way to the east toward Tepahlewam, where they had met just about three weeks before to enjoy their last days of freedom.

Again they were free to travel where they pleased. And they were now in a position to attack the supply trains from Fort Lapwai that furnished Howard's army with food and ammunition.

The deep canyon and the boiling waters at the second crossing of the Salmon River stopped the advance of Howard's troops. Since he had no rafts and no boats, he had no choice but to turn around and pass over the same cruel and terrifying mountain trail and suffer the same brutal hardships of the past four days.

From Tepahlewam the Nez Perces followed the familiar trails across Camas Prairie and into the valley of the Clearwater River. The travel was less difficult but it was more dangerous. On both sides of their route were farms and villages of frightened white settlers. The scouts kept watch, and small bands of warriors kept moving between the white people and the almost endless line of Nez Perces and their horses.

On the second day of the journey from the Salmon River, a warrior sighted and gave warning of a scouting party of ten soldiers and two volunteers led by a lesser white chief named Lieutenant Rains. Five Wounds with four other braves rode out to prevent this enemy band from causing any trouble.

The action was violent and short. Not one white man survived the attack. The warriors returned unhurt.

Another group of white scouts, seventeen in number, almost met the same fate. Two were killed and three were wounded before one hundred soldiers came to the rescue.

Owyeen, an older brave, was wounded in this fight. That night he died, the first warrior to lose his life in the Nez Perce War of 1877.

The white men in the towns were disgusted to learn that General Howard had failed to overtake the Nez Perces. And whenever they received the news that an army patrol had met a band of the warriors, it was only to hear of another defeat for the white men.

They decided to take action on their own. Eighty farmers, ranchers, and townspeople armed themselves and swung into their saddles. After being warned to beware of riding into a trap, they started off to show the soldiers how to fight the Indians.

Ollokot and his warriors drove these volunteers to the top of a high hill, and for a day and a night held them captive under fire. No one was injured, but the white men suffered greatly from thirst, exhaustion, and fear. The place of their long torture became known as Misery Hill.

At the camp on the Clearwater River, the bands of Nez Perces there were reunited with the bands of Looking Glass and Red Owl. Behind these two chiefs came another hundred women and children to be protected and cared for. They also brought with them forty very angry warriors who were looking for a fight with the white men.

Until the morning of July 1, about one week before, Looking Glass and his people had been living quietly in their village. They were bothering nobody. They had no intention of harming anyone. But on that morning, Captain Stephen Whipple with over a hundred troops appeared at the edge of the village. Looking Glass raised the white flag of peace. He sent a warrior to tell Whipple that he and his people were not at war with the white men. They felt no hatred or anger toward anyone. They wished only to be left alone.

But Looking Glass had refused to sign the Treaty of 1863. He had refused to move his people to the new reservation. He was therefore an enemy of the white men.

Whipple's soldiers opened fire with their cannons. Then, with rifles blazing, they charged the village.

The Indians ran to the woods and hills. Two were wounded and two were shot to death. In her terror a mother with her child threw herself into the river and the two were drowned.

The soldiers burned the houses and tepees. They rode their horses up and down over the gardens. They took possession of six hundred horses that belonged to Looking Glass and his band. The vegetable crops were trampled by the soldiers' horses and completely destroyed. The entire village of Looking Glass was now level with the crushed and worthless plants in their ruined gardens.

Out of sympathy for Looking Glass, Red Owl and his people had chosen to leave their land and fight with their Nez Perce brothers. Their homeland was within the borders of the new reservation, and the people could have remained there in peace.

Hearing Looking Glass's unhappy tale, Joseph, Too-hoolhoolzote, and many of the warriors wanted to take the war into the camps of the enemy. Those who were opposed to this had strong arguments in their favor. It was true that General Howard and his soldiers had again crossed the Salmon River, but they were still days of hard travel from the Nez Perce camp. The people were tired. The council had made no plans. Why not relax for a time? Give the council a chance to decide about their future. The scouts would report on the enemy's position and warn of an approach.

And so with relief they settled down to rest and enjoy themselves. They raced their horses, swam in the river, and loafed. When a scout came from the hill or the forest, he entered into the games and sports, and forgot that no one had replaced him. The tribe was caught off guard.

General Howard and his four hundred soldiers were very close when a warrior made the discovery. The white men were even then crowding to the very edge of the canyon cliffs above the Nez Perce camp. On command, the cannons were drawn up to the rim of the canyon, and the soldiers began to spread out in a line in readiness to descend the high steep canyon slopes.

On this hostile appearance of the enemy, the warriors calmly mounted their horses and received their rifles from the hands of the women. Then they dug their heels into the ribs of the horses, slackened the reins, and dashed off to seek positions of advantage to meet and stop the enemy.

The Nez Perces could bring to the field of battle less than two hundred warriors, with only about seventy armed with modern rifles. Yet they were not afraid to match their courage and military skill with the might of the white man's army. As old Chief Toohoolhoolzote never grew tired of reminding them, they might be weak in numbers, but they were strong in courage and skill. As horsemen and as riflemen, the warriors were far superior to the soldiers. Until then, their much smaller force had proved the equal of the army.

When the soldiers reached the level ground at the base of the canyon slopes, the warriors swept to the attack. They charged the end positions of the lines of troops, trying to separate the soldiers from one another so that the fewer warriors could fight a more equal number of the enemy. But the troops were too many. They could not be divided. They stood like a thick forest of solid trees. Even if one had wished to escape, he could not have moved because of the other soldiers on every side of him.

The fighting raged through the long and weary hours of that hot July afternoon. The warriors made their quick and daring assaults, and the soldiers held their ground. A mountain stream was the only nearby source of drinking water, and this became the cause of a fierce battle, neither side winning possession of it.

The Indians tried to capture an important supply train. They killed the white men who led the teams of horses, but a strong defense by the troops saved their supplies.

Darkness fell on six hundred dusty and tired men, with no one to claim and celebrate a victory.

During the night, the soldiers dug trenches, the better to hold their position the next day. The chiefs and warriors went into council.

White Bird advised them to prepare for a retreat. The

young braves received this suggestion as an insult. They had never known defeat, and their past success had made their proud hearts even bolder.

But the eye of the next sun saw a change in their fortunes. The soldiers seized and held the mountain stream. The men at the cannons had found the range of the Nez Perce camp and were punishing the women and children with their shells. General Howard rode among his troops, cheering and urging them on.

One by one, the warriors began to give up the fight. Joseph saw the danger. He ran to the people and told them to break camp and follow the river to the north.

The people escaped, but only by abandoning an abundance of their food supplies, camp equipment, and valuable personal belongings. They trailed northward, driving their horses before them.

For some reason, General Howard did not pursue them. When a scout informed Joseph that Howard was calling off his troops, he pushed on with the people in less of a hurry, but he did not let them rest until they had reached an old Nez Perce meeting place on Weippe Prairie.

Killed in the Battle of Clearwater River were four warriors and thirteen soldiers. Six braves and twenty-two white men were wounded.

The Nez Perces had experienced a serious blow from their powerful enemy. They had suffered a heavy loss of possessions. But not a word was spoken of surrender. At the camp on Weippe Prairie, the council met to answer one question: Were they to carry on the war or continue the retreat?

"The Wellamotkin are fighting for their right to return

Chief Joseph (seated right),
with other Nez Perces

to the Wallowa Valley," said Joseph. "For us there is no choice between war and retreat. Only by opposing the white man will we save our homeland."

White Bird spoke for many in the council when he said that they could not hope to win in this struggle with the white man. Their only hope was justice. They must defend themselves and save their livestock and pray that one day the white men would recognize and repent of the error and injustice of their actions.

Looking Glass advised that the Nez Perces cross the Lolo Trail into Montana. They had many friends in the buffalo country, the game was plentiful, and there was more than enough pasture land for their horses.

Joseph was alarmed to see that many in the council seemed to favor this suggestion. Speaking with deep feeling, he urged them to stay here in Idaho and make a stand against the thieves who, with their guns and fences, would steal the valleys and meadows, the grazing lands, the fishing streams and the hunting trails, all of which, since time began, had belonged to all men. His voice was like the thunder, his arguments swept the council like a storm, yet over half of the warriors voted to retreat beyond the Bitterroot Mountains into Montana.

And so began the journey that scholars have called one of the most difficult, most skillfully managed, and most courageous marches ever to be recorded in the pages of history.

CHAPTER V

Thorns
and Roses

The old men bundled up the tepee walls of buffalo hide. The young children held the horses' reins, and the boys fastened straps around the horses' bellies and tied the poles of the travois to the straps. The girls and women packed food supplies into baskets and placed the baskets on the travois. The mothers strapped their infants onto the backs of horses, along with the saddle bags that held their few possessions.

Some of the families were afraid to undertake the journey. The Lolo Trail was two hundred and fifty miles of danger and hardship. Every mile was at least seven thousand feet above sea level, where the air was thin and breathing difficult. The narrow trail snaked through thick dark forests, climbed to freezing mountain heights, followed ledges of mile-high cliffs, and plunged into black ravines filled with boulders and dead trees. Thorny brush and jagged rocks hampered every step of the way. For good reason, many of the Nez Perces chose to remain behind in Idaho and live on the reservation.

Each person decided for himself. The tribe was held together only by the bonds of friendship. No family or clan was kept within the larger group by fear or by force.

The same was true for each individual member of the band. At no time was a man required to stay with his wife or family against his will. And yet almost everyone remained with his people, and marriages usually lasted until death. The bonds of affection were strong and seldom broken.

There were many tears in parting. There were much more passionate expressions of sorrow for another reason. Whenever the tribe was faced with change and doubt of the future, it was a custom of the Nez Perces for the women to moan and weep as if the world were coming to an end.

But in truth, few were sorry about the change or fearful of the future. They thought with regret of their homeland, how it was now undefended, and how the earth, the mother of all life, would now suffer the sharp, cutting blades of the white man's plow. But their hearts had been hardened by the white man's law, a law of injustice, that encouraged the murder of the Indian and the theft of his land.

On the morning of the sixteenth day of July, 1877, Joseph mounted his horse and headed the long file of travelers across the prairie toward the first light of the new sun, and toward the shadowy opening in the distant mass of trees that was the western entrance to the Lolo Trail.

Spirits were lifted by the shouts and laughter of the excited and confident young braves, as they rode their prancing horses on every side, protecting the people from surprise by the enemy.

All during the day their eyes searched the trees in the forest where the brush grew thick along the trail, or where huge rocks lay in the ravines, or where the shadows of the high cliffs fell black in deep shelters that could hide the enemy. They kept their eyes roving along the mountain ledges, watching for the blanket signal of the scout.

All through the long night the warriors on guard waited motionless, silent, so their ears would catch the man-made wail of the coyote.

With the faintest light of dawn, the wakeful old men would start off through the chilly morning mist among the cold ashes of last night's campfires to rouse the others from their slumbers.

In all, they numbered about two hundred and fifty men

Nez Perce warriors,
photographed in 1906 by Major Lee Moorhouse

and twice that many women and children. The war parties from each band were headed by the leading warriors. The entire tribe was guided by the decisions of the council. But the daily movement along the trail depended on the knowledge and labor of the women. They had been educated in the difficulties of forest and mountain travel during the many years of moving between their winter homes in the valley and the mountain meadows for the spring and summer harvests. That education was a help to them, but still, to gather food for so large a crowd as this, on a narrow, overgrown, and rocky pathway through a mountain forest, demanded all their effort and every trick they knew. It required a constant search for wild vegetables, berries, and roots, and much hard labor in peeling the outer bark from the trees to uncover and strip the juicy bark beneath, which was a valuable source of food in this rough country.

Every day for ten long days, from the first light of dawn to the last rays of twilight, the tribe pressed forward with hardly a wasted moment to nurse their cuts or comfort their weary muscles. And their efforts were rewarded by an increasing distance between themselves and their enemy. Their terrible weariness was lessened a little by the promise of friendship and safety in the Bitterroot Valley. But the farther they traveled, the more precious their homeland became to them. The more vividly they remembered its treasures. The more beautiful it was pictured in their imaginations. They thought back to a pleasant afternoon beside a friendly stream, or a day spent loafing on the soft grass of a mountain meadow, with the blue sky above and the green valley stretching out below. If only they might live over again just one of those happy days! Well before the end of the trail, even the strongest of the grown boys, whose easy job it was to drive the herds of horses, were beginning to feel the need of a long pause to rest.

Their three thousand horses left a wide trail of trampled grass and broken twigs and branches. Now and again one of the handsome animals slipped and fell with the sharp and awful sound of a bone breaking. Then the people fell into sadness as for the death of a friend. They dearly loved their horses, and it grieved them to see one of the strong and beautiful creatures crippled in this way. The horse was unable to travel on and must be left to die where it had fallen. The people could only pray that the Great Spirit would soon let it fall into its last sleep. Even the bravest warrior lacked the heart to take its life and so end its suffering.

On the tenth day of their journey, the trail dropped steeply and then opened out far below into the great rumpled blanket of the Bitterroot Valley. The rolling hills and stands of trees by the winding rivers lay beneath a thin cloud. Waiting for them under that gray mist, so the Nez Perces believed, were rest and food and friendship.

That evening they reached Lolo Creek at the foot of the mountain and stopped for the night. They sat around the cooking fires until a late hour, enjoying the success of their venture.

Shortly after dawn the following morning, a scout rode into camp with the news that a band of the enemy was blocking their passage into the valley. Eight miles up the trail, a log fort had been built between the walls of the canyon. It was manned by thirty-five soldiers and two hundred volunteers.

The council sent warriors to search the forests and rocky ledges above the canyon. They must find another route into the valley.

Then Joseph, Looking Glass, and White Bird walked alone up the canyon trail to speak with the chief of the enemy war party. The white men were amazed to see them so proudly and fearlessly striding into the range of the more than two hundred rifles that were aimed at them. The chiefs did not stop until they were within ten steps of the white leader, Captain Charles Rawn.

Joseph told the captain that the Nez Perces would enter the Bitterroot Valley, in peace if they could, by fighting if they must.

The volunteers all lived in the valley and were very eager to keep the peace. But was Chief Joseph telling the truth? Were these Indians truly friendly?

Joseph answered that the Nez Perces had taken the Lolo Trail, where no white men lived and few were ever seen, for one reason only, and that was to avoid trouble.

This reply satisfied the volunteers. They left Captain Rawn and returned to their homes.

High above the cliffs of the canyon wall, the Nez Perces made their way slowly but surely around the soldiers and their log fort. Captain Rawn was helpless to stop them. His fort would become a joke and he would be called a fool. But all he could do was watch the passing parade of seven hundred people and three thousand horses as they descended the mountain slopes and entered the valley of the Bitterroot River.

Now the people traveled on at an easy pace, making camp early in the afternoon and spending the rest of the day in fishing, hunting, sports, and games. Gradually their health and strength and cheerful spirits returned.

Hophoponmi put on her long yellow dress of smooth, rich leather, with the belt around the waist and the fringe around the hem. The leather for her moccasins and leggings had been cut from the tough hide of an old bull elk, but her dress had been made from the soft skin of a mountain sheep that her father had slain to supply meat for a winter feast. Her hat was woven of Indian hemp and decorated with colored string. She wore it to protect her hair and to shade her eyes from the sun. It also attracted the eyes of the young men.

With a basket under her arm and a girl companion at her side, she went to look for berries and wild fruits and vegetables. Was it very strange that the fattest berries and the ripest fruits she could find were close to where the boys were racing their horses?

In all the next ten days they journeyed but little more than one hundred miles. So restful was the travel that the hardships of the war in Idaho and of the Lolo Trail could be remembered and talked about without anger.

Scouts rode out in advance of the tribe to tell the farmers and village people that the Nez Perces came in peace. The white people were relieved, and they promised their friendship and help to the Indians.

Two more days brought them to Big Hole Basin, a huge valley of grassy meadows, streams lined with willow trees, and hills covered with pines. So quiet and pleasant was that beautiful land, and so safe did it seem, that the warriors were tempted to lay down their arms, stretch out on the soft prairie grass, and dream that here was home.

CHAPTER VI

From the Garden
to the Grave

It was just before dawn on the ninth morning of August, the day after the tribe had made camp on Beaver Creek in the Big Hole Basin. The women left their tepees to tend the dying campfires. They talked quietly together while they stirred the embers and added fresh fuel. When the fires were blazing again, they returned to their beds.

As the morning light began to turn the hills from black to gray, old Natalekin came from his tepee and made his way to where his horse was tied to a willow tree. He mounted and started off on a short ride in the pleasant coolness and calm of the early hour.

His eyesight was dim with age, and he was upon the four white men before he saw the danger. He did not have time to shout a warning. The people in the camp were aroused by the explosions from the rifles that killed old Natalekin.

Immediately, the west bank of Beaver Creek swelled up into one long wave of savage shouts and violent motion. One hundred and eighty soldiers and volunteers, with their rifles firing, came running across the stream toward the Nez Perce village.

The Indians had been awakened only the moment before.

Chief Joseph's home in 1901,
photographed by Major Lee Moorhouse

They were still lying down in the tepees or just leaving their beds. The white men had planned on this. They aimed their rifles toward the bottoms of the tepee walls.

Warriors rushed out through the tepee openings. Others came out limping or crawling. Women followed, leading and supporting injured old men, other women, boys, and girls. Mothers appeared holding babies and small children who were covered with blood and screaming with pain.

In their haste to get the women and children away to safety, the warriors left their weapons in the tepees. They banded together and formed a shield between their families and the white men. They fought with stones, clubs, knives, and their bare hands.

In the first minutes of the attack, Joseph's wife was killed. Quickly, he grabbed up the new baby girl and gave her to Hophoponmi. He told Hophoponmi to go to her aunt, Fair-land, Ollokot's wife, and with her seek the cover of the willow trees or the hills. The woman and the girl with the infant child were running to safety when Fair-land was struck down. Hophoponmi stopped but an instant, then ran on. She hid in the trees with her baby sister and then later escaped to the better protection of the hills.

With their wives both dead, Joseph and Ollokot gave themselves up to the grim and bloody action. They fought in silence, furiously and with great daring.

As the people retreated, the enemy began to move in. The soldiers tried to set fire to the tepees. The poles were new and green and the leather walls were wet with dew. Nothing would burn, yet the soldiers kept on in their hope of destroying the village with fire.

Now the warriors saw their chance. Hurriedly they searched the other tepees, found rifles and bows and arrows, and passed them to the braves waiting outside. Those who were armed with the weapons then dashed off to the bushes, the tall grass, and the trees. Then the marksmen began to level their deadly aim upon the enemy.

Other warriors continued the close fighting in the village. Looking Glass rushed everywhere, barking commands. Toohoolhoolzote bellowed like a maddened buffalo. Chief White Bird, in spite of his age, moved through the thick of the action with words of encouragement, advice, and caution. Now and then he drew his ancient bow and sent off an arrow with stinging accuracy.

Rainbow and Five Wounds were brought down at last. The braves who saw them fall were shocked and saddened. They had always believed that old age was the only enemy that could take the lives of those mightiest of warriors.

Wah-lait-its saw his wife die. In the terrible rage of his vengeance, he met his death. Then one of his companions, furious at the loss of his friend, charged the enemy and was killed.

Many other warriors lost their lives as Wah-lait-its and his friend had died, grief and anger driving them to avenge the death of a loved one.

The marksmen in the hills, woods, and tall prairie grass finally drove the white men away to the shelter of the rocks on a far hillside.

Joseph could hardly believe the horrors of the scene. Surely something was wrong with the minds of the white men. They had murdered over fifty women and children. Their purpose was truly evil. They wished to wipe the Nez Perce tribe, every last man, woman, and child, from the face of the earth.

Not a single family escaped with everyone still alive. Some families had only a single survivor. Other families had been completely wiped out. And every chief felt as though all the misery of his band had been gathered together and laid upon his heart.

The people returned to the village to bury the dead. There was no time to mourn. The scouts had reported that other soldiers were coming to rescue the troops who were trapped on the hill.

How the bitter experience changed the women! Would the girl still follow the example of her mother? Then she would not grow into a cheerful, sweet, and gentle Nez Perce woman. Her mother's face now seemed carved in stone. Her soft voice had turned sharp and cold. Her warm dark eyes had grown bold and hard in her grief and hatred.

The tribe moved southward through the Big Hole Valley. They traveled slowly, caring for their many wounded.

An advance party of scouts stopped at deserted farms and searched the houses for cloth material that could be used for bandages. At one place they were opposed by seven white men. The warriors killed five, chased away the other two, and took with them two hundred and fifty head of the white men's horses.

A hunting party of warriors came upon a train of wagons and pack mules. The warriors demanded the supplies. The white men refused, and they lost their lives.

The chiefs begged the warriors to cool their tempers. The angry man could not think clearly. Anger made a fire in the heart and filled the head with smoke.

But the warriors were deaf to the warnings of danger. Until now, they had been defending their families in the hope of returning one day to their homeland. Now this hope was gone. They felt only a passionate desire to save at least some of the people, if only a single family, to pre-serve their customs, their traditions, their old way of life.

Before the attack at Big Hole Basin, the warriors who had died fighting could be counted on the fingers of two hands. In that battle, thirty-three braves were lost. Thirty-four white men had been killed and forty-four wounded. Yet the loss to the Nez Perces was far greater. It was the soldier's job to kill or be killed. And he could be replaced. The warrior was fighting to save himself and his family. And he could not be replaced.

Word of the battle spread to the western towns, then to the cities in the East and the Southwest, so that from coast to coast the white men learned of the Battle of Big Hole Basin. At that time and in later years, scholars of the world's armies and their wars said that the fight at Big Hole Basin was one of the fiercest battles in all of military history.

In the days following that engagement, the white men of the area became very alarmed. They feared the revenge of the Nez Perces. Their fears grew and grew until they were calling for their government to put all of the Indians in the country to death. The Indians, they said, were a threat to the nation. Only the year before, General Custer had been defeated by Chief Sitting Bull at the Battle of Little Bighorn River.

But the fame of the long-suffering yet gentle Nez Perces also spread far and wide. Their warriors were so greatly outnumbered, yet they refused to surrender. Many white men had only praise and sympathy for such a courageous people.

On the twentieth of August, eleven days after the Battle of Big Hole Basin, the Nez Perces were camped on a hilly grassland called Camas Meadow. Toward evening, a scout rode into the camp and informed them that General Howard had crossed the Lolo Trail and was again in full command of the troops in the field. His soldiers were now less than one day of easy riding from the camp.

The council voted to move at once, now, tonight. Joseph

objected to this hasty decision. They were asking the people to break camp when only a few hours ago they had pitched their tepees.

"But the enemy is nearly upon us," said the old men. "Our weapons and warriors are too few to outfight General Howard's mighty army. Our women and children, our wounded braves, they are too many for us to outrun the soldiers on horseback."

"Then we must outsmart them," said Joseph.

The council listened carefully as Joseph explained his plan. Under cover of the night, the warriors would steal into the enemy camp, stampede and, if possible, capture the army's pack horses and mules. It was a daring scheme, but the chiefs approved, and the eager warriors ran for their horses and rifles.

Joseph held the reins while Ollokot mounted his horse. Ollokot was brave but often reckless, and Joseph was afraid for him.

"Fair-land is dead," said Ollokot. "I go now to fight for you and your two daughters. You are my family now."

"Then you must be careful. You must live to go on fighting," Joseph said.

Ollokot reined his horse around, nudged its belly with his heels, and galloped off across the prairie.

One by one the warriors of his party formed their horses in a line behind him. Another war party, with Toohoolhoolzote in the lead, started out a moment later on the same path.

The warriors who remained at camp spaced themselves in a circle of protection around the tepees. Joseph took up a position facing the enemy only eight miles away.

Through the long night he waited, patiently watching for the war parties to return, and standing ready should the enemy appear instead.

CHAPTER VII

Defeat
without Dishonor

The sky turned gray and then a pale blue. Joseph's long shadow darkened as the sun rose behind him. Slowly the light moved westward over the hills and on across the wide stretch of grassland, not stopping until it reached the tops of the low hills on the distant horizon.

Now Joseph could see men on horseback. He strained to make out whether the riders were soldiers or warriors. Then he saw the large herd that they were driving before them, and he breathed a sigh of relief. The animals came charging across the prairie with the fright and fury of a stampede.

Yellow Wolf rode ahead of Ollokot's war party to bring Joseph the news. Breathlessly he told how they had captured the enemy's pack mules, but that they had been discovered, and this very minute a hundred troops or more were racing after the Indian raiders and toward the Nez Perce camp.

Joseph sent runners to arouse the people and to tell the older boys to prepare to ride.

As the herd of two hundred mules thundered past, the boys leaped upon their ponies and dashed off in pursuit. The warriors who had been stampeding the herd then reined about and galloped into camp. They turned their horses over to the women and ran with their rifles into the hills and tall grass where other braves already lay in hiding.

Joseph made sure that Ollokot had returned with the warriors, then he rode off with Chief White Bird to the head of the long slow column of people, their horses, and General Howard's two hundred mules.

General Howard and his army were at a standstill. He could send out war parties of soldiers, but the main body of his troops, with all their cannons and heavy crates of ammunition and equipment, could not march on without the teams of mules to pull the wagons. He could do nothing but wait until his soldiers could recover the herd that the Nez Perces had captured, or until his agents could locate, purchase, and drive another herd into his camp.

The soldiers raced after the thieving Indians, but were halted by a shower of arrows and a blast of rifle fire. For four hours they were held up there on the prairie, while the tribe retreated with the stolen mules.

The Nez Perces hurried on eastward toward Targhee Pass, one of the entrances through the mountains into Yellowstone National Park. Just five years before, in 1872, the land for this park had been set aside for the enjoyment of all white people. These thirty-five hundred square miles, over two million acres, were owned by the entire nation of white people. The land could not be sold or fenced. Everyone was free to travel anywhere within the boundaries of the park.

This gave the Indians another reason to question the wisdom of the white men. The white men protected the park land for the pleasure of all, yet they could not understand why the Indians believed that the land of the whole earth should be free for all men to enjoy.

General Howard learned the route of the Nez Perces and sent a war party to block Targhee Pass. But the young leader of this party grew impatient while he waited there, and left in the hope of attacking his Indian foe. The tribe entered the park without an argument.

They camped on the banks of the Madison River. This river well repaid the skill and patience of the fishermen. Hunger had long tormented the people. Now a large catch of fish helped to ease this suffering, and gave to many of the very old and very young the strength to go on.

But they could pause only for the night. If they stopped any longer, the enemy would overtake them.

Their war parties came upon groups of tourists in the park. The meetings were often unpleasant, for the white men could not be trusted. Even those who were friendly, once they were safe from harm, ran at once to the white leaders and informed them of the position and route of the Nez Perces.

With each breakup of the night's camp and with each day's travel, the Nez Perces improved the strategy of their retreat. From dawn to dark and from dark to dawn, the scouts watched from the ledges of rock high up on the steep mountain cliffs. With the red blanket and the cry of the coyote, they reported the movements of the soldiers. With these signals and by cunning and trickery, they kept the distance of a day's ride between themselves and their enemy.

The soldiers were completely fooled. Again and again the army scouts brought the encouraging news that the Nez

Perces had been sighted and the officer gave the order to ride, but every hopeful chase ran them into a dead end.

The Nez Perces were challenged by the almost limitless resources in men, supplies, and weapons of the United States army. Marching in this army were veterans of many actions of past wars. These veterans had defeated the Mexicans, warred against other Indian tribes, and fought each other in the war that had divided their nation. General Howard had lost his left arm at the Battle of Fair Oaks in the American Civil War, which had ended only twelve years before. Colonel Samuel Sturgis had taken part in every type of conflict and was an experienced Indian fighter.

The Nez Perces first met Sturgis in the northeast corner of Yellowstone Park. In less than a day they could have passed through Clark Fork Canyon and left the park for the country of the friends, the Crow Indians, to the north, but Sturgis and his troops stood in the way. And General Howard with his army was moving up from behind. On both sides of them were other, smaller war parties of white men. On the eighth day of September, after two weeks of hide-and-seek in Yellowstone Park with their enemy, the Nez Perces discovered that they were surrounded. They were caught in a trap.

The chiefs and leading warriors quickly formed the council circle. Joseph's position in the tribe was now that of guide and protector of all the people who were not engaged in warfare. He was their leader on the trail. He chose the place and hour to camp for the night. At all times he must think of their safety. The problem now was more serious than any he had faced before. The enemy threatened his people on every side. He asked for the advice of the chiefs and warriors.

A brave stepped forward to speak. He said that he had hunted in this area and was familiar with it. He offered a plan that he believed would fool the white men and permit the Nez Perces to escape.

With this brave riding beside him and pointing the direction, Joseph swung about and led the people down a dark trail through heavy forests and between high hills. Sturgis thought the Indians were heading for a southern exit from the park. He and his soldiers galloped off to block this route.

The Nez Perces again reversed their direction. Clark Fork Canyon was unguarded now. It was a narrow, over-grown, and rocky passage, hardly a trail at all, but they struggled through. Seven hundred Indians with three thousand horses escaped from the white man's national park and the soldiers' trap.

They were out in the open now, and the travel was easier. The next day's retreat increased by fifty miles the distance from the enemy. But still they could not relax either their guard or their pace. Sturgis was shamed and angered by their trick. They had slipped out of his grasp, and he vowed that he and his soldiers would stay in their saddles until the Nez Perces had paid for making a fool out of him.

To his own one hundred troops were added three hundred from General Howard's force. With these and two large cannons besides, he spurred his horse to its utmost speed, and ordered his soldiers to do the same.

Not far ahead of the Nez Perces was the mouth of

Canyon Creek. The valley of this small stream, though wide and flat for most of its length, became in places a narrow, stony trail with steep canyon walls. These narrow places offered a way of slowing down the rapid pursuit of Sturgis's war party.

The people entered the valley, and in back of them the warriors took up positions in the tall prairie grass, behind large rocks, and among the hills. There were more than twice as many soldiers, but the strength of the warriors was doubled by the enemy's fear of their accurate rifle fire.

As the people moved into the valley, the warriors followed them, backing away from the advancing troops. They delayed the soldiers until nightfall. By then the people had reached the hills beyond the valley. At the places where the sides of the valley came close together, the last warriors who passed through pulled down brush and rocks into the narrow canyon floor, making it impossible to travel the trail in the dark.

The people searched the horizon for signs of the Crows. Their scouts rode out to look for this friendly tribe. Crow warriors did return with the Nez Perce scouts, but not as friends. They came to make war on the Nez Perces, to raid their camp and steal their horses. The Crows were scouting and fighting for the white man's army.

The Nez Perces had traveled far. For nearly a hundred days they had followed the trail, and how very few had been their days of peace and rest! In the trials of each day and the weariness of each night, they had forgotten to fear the future.

Shelter, food, and help from their brothers, the Crows, had been their hope. To find them enemies was a bitter blow. Worse than false brothers, the Crows were no better than animals, for they had turned against their own people and friends to follow the white thieves and murderers. They were like the coyotes that trail the cougar to feed off the scraps of the kill after the cougar has devoured his fill.

The Nez Perces must travel on. The enemy was snapping at their heels.

Their last hope was Canada. Sitting Bull had made his new home there, where the agents of the United States government could not reach him. Surely he and his people would welcome these Nez Perces, for they too had refused the life of the reservation.

Much of the land was flat prairie now. For long distances the travelers were visible for miles, exposed to attack by day and to a surprise assault by night. Their only protection was to keep a safe distance between themselves and the enemy.

Food supplies were running short. The fishermen could promise nothing. There was little time for picking berries and digging roots. The hunting parties seldom returned with enough fresh meat to feed everyone, and the portions were always small.

The children looked up at their mothers hopefully. Babies sighed and whimpered. These were the only signs that the evil of hunger was among them. But the hunger was painful for everyone, and it was getting worse. Yet not one voice spoke a single word of surrender.

They knew that the white man would kill his horse for food. But to the Indian, the horse was a friend and companion. Even during the worst periods of their starvation, nobody gave even a passing thought to killing these animals.

At noon on the twenty-third of September, fourteen days and three hundred and fifty miles from Yellowstone Park, they arrived at Cow Island Landing on the Missouri River. This was the last steamboat landing up the river from the east. From here, supplies for the trading posts and forts farther west had to be transported by wagons and pack-horses.

Provisions had been unloaded from steamboats only a few days before. The Nez Perces first offered to pay for the food that they so desperately needed. When the white men refused the offer, the warriors held them off with rifles while the women and old men loaded their horses with boxes and sacks of food supplies.

They pushed onward to the north. Winter comes early in this part of the country, and they began to feel and to fear the wind that swept down from the snowy mountain peaks. This dreadful, invisible monster dashed across the ice-coated shelves of rock, through the shaded, dark, and frozen ravines, and attacked them without mercy, robbing their strength during the day and their sleep at night. During the next six days, they covered less than fifty miles.

The scouts kept their careful watch. Wrapped in blankets to their eyes, they searched the great reach of the prairie and the cold depths of the hills beyond. By night they searched for a sign — the flare of a lighted match, the sparkle of moonlight on a brass button, a movement against the deep gray of the sky. For three days and nights they reported no sign of the enemy.

By the twenty-ninth of September, they had reached the northern edge of the mountain range called Bear Paw, just forty miles, one day's long journey, from the Canadian border. Here a hunting party sighted a herd of buffalo. Chief Looking Glass urged the council to allow the tribe to stop for a day or two of rest, and to eat their fill after traveling so far and so long with that other hateful monster, hunger.

Early the following day, two scouts raced into the camp, shouting that a large band of the enemy was riding toward them. The eyes of the young warriors flashed with eagerness. The old veterans of the hunt and the warpath moved without emotion to prepare for the coming battle.

The women with infants and small children hurried to mount their horses. About a hundred of them, protected by sixty warriors, escaped north to Canada.

The eyes of every other woman and child were fixed with terror on the swift approach of the lines of smoke and the steady explosions of fire, as the enemy stormed down upon them.

In this enemy band were six hundred soldiers led by Colonel Nelson Miles. Miles was the commander at Fort Keogh, two hundred miles to the east. Twelve days before, he had received a message from General Howard, ordering him to block the flight of the Nez Perces to Canada. Miles and his men had set out at once on a rapid march. Early on the last morning of September, he sent his troops in a furious charge against the Nez Perce camp.

The lines of troopers on horseback rushed down upon the Indians with the swiftness and thunder of an avalanche. The warriors held their fire until the enemy horsemen were well within the range of their rifles. Then the soldiers received the deadly volley from the Nez Perce marksmen.

The enemy's lines were broken, and the attack was

halted. For a time the close combat was very mixed and confused. Then the struggle began to prove too costly for the white men. Colonel Miles ordered the soldier with the trumpet to blow the sound of retreat.

As the soldiers pulled back, they formed a wide circle around the Nez Perces. The Indians were surrounded, but then the white men themselves were also captives, pinned down in their trenches by the sure aim of the Nez Perce riflemen.

The Battle of Bear's Paw lasted five days. In all, twenty-five Nez Perces and twenty-three white men were killed; forty-six Nez Perces and forty-five soldiers were wounded. Nearly all who fell in the battle did so in the first seconds of the attack and the fighting of that first day. The mighty chief Toohoolhoolzote lost his life in this brief space of time. So did the mighty warrior Ollokot, Joseph's brother.

On the second day, a messenger from Colonel Miles walked toward the Nez Perce camp. He carried the white flag of truce. Joseph went out to meet him. The messenger invited the Nez Perce chief to speak with the chief of the white man's army. Perhaps they could come to an agreement that would prevent further bloodshed. Joseph followed the messenger behind the enemy's line. The moment he entered Miles's camp, he was seized and placed under the guard of many soldiers.

Joseph remembered how the missionaries used to say that the white man's success in war and on the hunt and with farming was due to the special favor of the Great Father Above. Why then had it been necessary for Colonel Miles to violate the white flag of truce?

Miles demanded that Joseph surrender. Joseph replied

that he and his people hoped to return to their beautiful Wallowa Valley, there to know again the pleasure of the glad heart when it was free. If they were to lose this hope, then their lives would be of no value to them. Then they would fight until all were destroyed.

Miles was so eager to claim the defeat of the Nez Perces as a victory for himself that he promised Joseph and his people a safe journey back to Idaho. If they surrendered now, he said, they could spend the winter at Fort Keogh and then return to the Wallowa Valley in the spring.

Joseph asked him to repeat the promise, and Miles did so. Again, Joseph asked to hear the promise repeated, and Miles answered as Joseph wished. It was a belief of the Nez Perces that when a man said the same words three times, his listener could be certain that he spoke honestly.

Then Joseph said that first he must speak with the other chiefs and warriors. Only the entire council could decide so important a matter as surrender.

But Miles would not release Joseph. He refused to part with so valuable a prize.

Two days later, Nez Perce warriors captured a lesser chief of the white man's army. This prisoner was exchanged for Joseph.

Back at the Nez Perce camp, Joseph was saddened by the suffering of the people. Thorns and brambles had torn their clothing to rags. All were weak from hunger, illness, and the freezing cold.

Fear had always been a stranger to Joseph's spirit, but his heart could not shut out the pity he felt for his people. He advised the council to accept the white man's terms of surrender.

But Chief Looking Glass could not trust in Miles's offer of shelter and food for the coming winter. Nor could Chief White Bird believe the promise that in the spring the Nez Perces would be allowed to return as a free people to their ancient homes in Idaho.

Suddenly a warrior at the edge of the camp raised his voice in a loud cheer. He shouted for all to look toward the north. There upon a distant hill was the movement of many animals. Joseph had sent a scout to find the village of Chief Sitting Bull and to ask for his help. It was possible that the scout was now returning with a war party from Sitting Bull.

Looking Glass jumped up and ran to see for himself. A bullet from a soldier's rifle struck him in the forehead. He was killed instantly. The animals on the hill were buffalo.

Old Chief White Bird and his band, under cover of darkness, departed for Canada. Joseph persuaded Hophoponmi to go along with White Bird. On their journey, they met Sitting Bull's warriors riding south to join the Nez Perces in their war with the white men. But they were too late. Joseph had presented his rifle to the white chiefs as a token of his surrender.

In front of the white men, Joseph stood tall and straight and proud. His clothing was ripped by bullet holes. Bullets had left scars on his forehead, his wrists, and his back. The sufferings of his people weighed heavily upon his heart. The deaths of his wife and his brother lay like two cold stones upon his spirit. Yet never did he bow his head to these white men. Never did his expression or posture so much as hint of his weariness and sorrow.

When he spoke, his voice was quiet and calm. And his words are among the most famous of all such speeches of surrender:

Tell General Howard I know his heart. What he told me before, I have it in my heart. I am tired of fighting. Our chiefs are killed. Looking Glass is dead. Toohoolhoolzote is dead. The old men are all dead. It is the young men who say yes or no. He who led the young men is dead. It is cold, and we have no blankets. The little children are freezing to death. My people, some of them, have run away to the hills, and have no blankets, no food. No one knows where they are — perhaps freezing to death. I want to have time to look for my children, and see how many of them I can find. Maybe I shall find them among the dead. Hear me, my chiefs. I am tired. My heart is sick and sad. From where the sun now stands I will fight no more forever.

Joseph's people were herded aboard fourteen flat-bottomed boats and shipped down the Missouri River to Kansas. There they were placed on a reservation, where they remained until a hundred had died of grief and homesickness. Almost all the newborn babies died because their mothers were too ill to care for them. Many of the older children also died. Joseph's second daughter, who had been born on the eve of the Nez Perce War of 1877, died before her fifth year of life. The people were finally moved to Indian Territory in Oklahoma, but their condition was improved very little.

Joseph journeyed to Washington, D.C. He met the

president and other high officials of the white man's government. He pleaded for his people. The climate of Oklahoma was unhealthy for them, and they were dying of disease. And they were dying of heartache, for where they now lived there were no mountains, meadows, rivers, or forests.

At last, in 1885, about a hundred Nez Perces were taken

Historical marker at Bear's Paw Battleground

to Lapwai reservation in Idaho. The remaining Indians were thought to be too dangerous to live so close to the land of their birth. They were settled on the Colville reservation in Washington Territory, some one hundred and fifty miles to the north of Fort Lapwai, two hundred miles north of the Wallowa Valley. Joseph was one of them.

Both Chief Joseph and Nelson Miles were born in 1840. In 1900, Colonel Miles was advanced to the rank of lieutenant general of the United States army.

Four years later, far from his home, the land of his birth and his father's grave, far from his beloved Wallowa Valley, Joseph died.

The doctor at the Colville Indian agency had to write up a report of Joseph's death. His report had to include the name of the person who had died, and the hour, the day, the place, and, finally, the cause of his death. The doctor quickly filled in all of the details except the last. Then he hesitated. What was the cause, the real cause of Joseph's death?

The doctor knew the history of 1877. It was almost thirty years ago now, and the white man's fear of the Indians had passed. His victory had been won. His desire for this rich and beautiful land had encouraged him to believe many falsehoods about the Indian, but most of the lies had passed away with his fear. And the doctor remembered the stories that he had heard about the courageous Nez Perces, of their hope and struggle to save their homeland, then of their honorable and masterful but melancholy flight to save their people.

The doctor paused in thought a moment longer. Then he dipped his pen in ink, and he wrote that Joseph, chief

Chief Joseph,
1901 photograph by Major Lee Moorhouse

"Chief Joseph"
NezPerce Tribe

Copyright-1901
by
Lee Moorhouse

of the Wellamotkin band of the Numipu tribe, a brave warrior, a resourceful leader, and a wise statesman, born free but for nearly half his life a prisoner of reservation boundaries, had died of "a broken heart."

Photo by Robert Wilcox

THE AUTHOR

R. P. Johnson is a native of Minnesota
and a graduate of the University of
Minnesota. His early interest was theater,
as an actor and playwright. Since then
he has written fiction (a novel, *Legacy
of Thorns,* appeared in 1965), book
reviews, and criticsm. He is also the
author of *Osceola: The Story of an
American Indian.* Mr. Johnson has
worked as an editor and a historian, and
has taught high school in Idaho, Michigan,
and Minnesota. In 1971, he received a
fellowship from the Edward MacDowell
Colony for artists in New Hampshire.
He is currently living in Minnesota,
occupied with writing and with continued
study of his primary interest, literature.

*The photographs are reproduced through
the courtesy of the Montana Department
of Highways, Smithsonian Institution,
U. S. Army Museum at Fort Sill, and
W. H. Over Museum at the University of
South Dakota.*

BIOGRAPHIES IN
THIS SERIES ARE

Joseph Brant
Crazy Horse
Geronimo
Chief Joseph
King Philip
Osceola
Powhatan
Red Cloud
Sacajawea
Chief Seattle
Sequoyah
Sitting Bull
Tecumseh
William Warren
William Beltz
Robert Bennett
LaDonna Harris
Oscar Howe
Maria Martinez
Billy Mills
George Morrison
Michael Naranjo
Maria Tallchief
James Thorpe
Pablita Velarde
Annie Wauneka